COUNTRY LIVING
MAGAZINE

Garden Wisdom

Garden Wisdom

SHARON AMOS

FOLKFORE AND FACT FOR MAKING YOUR GARDEN GROW

COLLINS & BROWN

First published in 2005
by Collins & Brown Limited
The Chrysalis Building
Bramley Road
London W10 6SP

An imprint of **Chrysalis** Books Group plc

Published in association with The National
Magazine Company Limited.
Country Living is a trade mark of The National
Magazine Company Limited.

1 3 5 7 9 8 6 4 2

British Library Cataloguing-in-Publication Data:
A catalogue record for this book is available
from the British Library.

ISBN 1 84340 265 3

Conceived, edited and designed by Collins &
Brown Limited

Project Editor: Carly Madden

Designer: Penny Stock

Reproduction by Classic Scan Ltd, Singapore

Printed and bound by Times, Malaysia

Contents

Welcome to Garden Wisdom – an inspiring mix of practical advice, traditional garden lore and eco-friendly ideas from Country Living Magazine compiled to help you make the most of your garden.

According to Elizabethan philosopher and essayist Francis Bacon, a garden is the 'the purest of human pleasures. It is the greatest refreshment to the spirits of man'. As anyone who has one will confirm, a garden can indeed seem like a piece of heaven on earth – a haven of peace and tranquillity which soothes the soul and provides relief from the pressures of our busy, modern lives.

This book tells you the essentials about the preparation, cultivation and maintenance of a garden, be it large or small, lawn or terrace, or even just a windowbox, and provides indispensable advice both for fairweather gardeners and for those who garden at every opportunity, whatever the weather. I hope you will find Garden Wisdom an invaluable companion all year round.

Susy Smith

Susy Smith

Editor, Country Living Magazine

Introduction

There is always something new to unearth about gardening – no matter how long you've been a gardener or how many gardens you've tended. You never stop learning: fellow gardeners, friends and neighbours pass on hints and ideas, while snippets of useful information turn up in magazines and newspapers.

This book is packed with garden wisdom, and not just traditional tips and ideas, but some very new research, too.

What links all the information gathered here is that every idea is simple, is easily achievable and really does produce results.

The book is divided into four broad sections: earth, air, water and plant alchemy. Earth begins at grassroots level, so to speak, and covers everything from newfangled ways of making compost to tips for ageing terracotta. The section on Air deals with topics as varied as plants that thrive in shade, how to create an old-fashioned hot bed in a greenhouse and how best to store garden produce. It unveils simple ways to beat unseasonable frosts or, at the very least, minimize damage, and reminds us of country lore for predicting weather.

Water considers ways of preserving what is fast becoming our most precious resource and how to use it effectively in the garden. There are tips for making a pond, and advice on both water-loving and drought-resistant plants.

Finally, Plant Alchemy begins with the art of companion planting – where one species appears to protect another against insect attack or disease. This chapter also offers the opportunity for a nostalgic glimpse of the all-but-forgotten Victorian language of flowers.

The Garden Shed

At its most functional, a shed is simply a tool store; at its most romantic, it is a private retreat. Of course, most sheds also have to double as places to store bikes, folding furniture and the lawnmower. They therefore tend to be a mixture of the two, catering both for storage and for the need to escape, with just enough space for an old chair.

Storing Tools and Vegetables

The easiest way to keep tools to hand is to hang them on pegs. This way, it's obvious at a glance what is in use or just plain missing. An old bookcase or set of shelves can hold small but essential pieces of equipment, such as garden twine, cane caps, scissors, plant labels, plant ties, as well as the inevitable old paint tins.

A corner of the shed can also double as a vegetable store. As it is likely to escape frost, you can safely hang up strings of onions and garlic, tuck away sacks of potatoes and stack wooden trays of apples if you have room. Just keep an eye open for hungry mice and for any ill effects of damp.

Instant Interest

Climbing plants soften stark outlines and veil a less than beautiful shed. By all means plant a rose or clematis, but while it is getting established, use rapid-growing annual species like the cup-and-saucer vine (*Cobaea scandens*) with its curious flowers – it can grow 1.5 m (5 ft) in a summer. Chilean glory vine (*Eccremocarpus scaber*) provides instant colour and camouflage.

Garden Tools

The Bare Minimum

The truth is that you can manage with as many or as few tools as you like, depending mostly on the size of your plot and what you are intending to grow. If you have a vegetable plot, then a spade, a fork, a shovel and a hoe will be essential, along with a garden line to mark off rows, a dibble for

planting out everything from beans to leek seedlings and a wheelbarrow to cart manure wherever it is needed.

In a densely planted flower garden, it is possible to manage with a trowel, a small border fork and a pair of secateurs (pruning shears). When the need arises, improvisation is the key – kitchen scissors cut sweet peas easily, while a garden fork can double as a rake.

Care of Metal Tools

To remove rust from the blades of secateurs (pruning shears), loppers or any other metal tools, rub with a scouring pad dipped in lighter fuel. This is also useful to clean blades after pruning conifers with sticky resin or the sappy growth of shrubs. Wipe the blades with a soft cloth to finish and put the tools away in the tool shed – don't leave them lying around outside. A squirt of WD40 or similar spray lubricant will keep the spring mechanism working well. Some hardware stores and garden centres offer blade-sharpening services. Don't neglect wooden handles either: keep them clean and, once a year, sand the wood lightly and rub in some boiled linseed oil.

Garden Furniture

A garden is incomplete without somewhere to sit and admire the fruits and flowers of your labour. Even if you are quite sure you will never have time to sit on it, think of a bench instead as a focal point, surrounded by plants. Matching form to the style of garden will make sure that furniture sits comfortably in the landscape.

Painting Furniture

Household gloss paint is fine for painting both wooden and metal folding chairs, and it will last reasonably well if the furniture is stored under cover in winter. For best results, sand and prime surfaces first. Leftover emulsion (latex) paint can be used to brighten up chairs and tables if you add a final protective coat of varnish – yacht varnish is ideal.

Deckchairs

The canvas 'sling' of an old deckchair can become thin and worn, especially where it has rubbed against the wooden frame, but it's easy enough to replace. Pull out the upholstery tacks with a claw hammer and measure the length of the sling, then buy a replacement length of tough canvas from a DIY store or the fabric department of a department store. Nail it to the frame with new tacks. Modern deckchairs often come with detachable slings so that you change the chair's appearance to suit the occasion.

earth

Soil Type

Soil is formed by centuries of frost, wind and rain wearing away the bedrock of the land. Along with these minute rock particles, the decaying remains of plants and animals contribute to the soil's structure, which in turn is home to millions of micro-organisms. Algae, bacteria, fungi, worms and insects all make up a teeming community critical to the soil's health.

Sandy Soil

Soil on sandstone bedrock is dry and light. If you pick up a handful and let it run through your fingers, it feels gritty – sandy, in fact – indicating its free-draining nature. Sandy soil tends to run out of nutrients quickly, as they are leached away with rainwater. Adding plenty of compost or well-rotted manure is a good way to counterbalance this tendency. As well as providing nutrients, the organic matter bulks up the soil structure and slows down drainage.

Chalky Soil

The topsoil on a chalk ridge tends to be shallow and often stony, studded with great flints. The soil is pale in colour and free-draining; once again, lots of well-rotted manure is needed to improve water and nutrient retention. Chalk tends to be very alkaline, and organic matter adds acidity, creating a more workable balance. Where the soil is particularly shallow, it may be sensible to buy in some good-quality topsoil to build it up.

Clay Soil

Clay is a heavy, sticky soil, waterlogged in winter and baked hard as a rock in summer. The same solution applies – add plenty of manure and compost – but in this case to open up the soil and improve drainage. The raw soil can seem intractable and digging can be disheartening work, but after several years of manuring and cultivating, this becomes one of the best soils to grow on.

Soil Acidity

The fertility of soil is directly affected by how acidic or alkaline it is. When soil is too acid, certain nutrients essential for growth become 'locked' in the soil and thus unavailable to plants. Acid soils prevent plants from taking up calcium, and significantly reduce the amounts of nitrogen, phosphorus and potassium they can absorb. Similarly, very alkaline soils lock up nitrogen, phosphorus and potassium.

For the best results, the soil needs to be neutral – somewhere between pH 6.5 and 7. It is relatively easy to adjust soil pH: digging well-rotted manure or garden compost, both of which are acidic, into alkaline soil can bring the pH down towards neutral. In the majority of cases, soil is too acidic and this can be corrected by adding slaked lime (alkaline), or spent mushroom compost, which contains lime.

Determining Soil Type

If you like gadgets, by all means use a proper soil-testing kit to determine your soil's pH, but you may not get an accurate overall picture, as pockets of soil can vary considerably. In fact, there is a much simpler method that gives a truer indication of soil acidity – it consists of just looking around at the plants that thrive in your garden and in your neighbours' plots.

Magnificent camellias, rhododendrons and beds of heather point to the earth being acidic, as these species are all lime-hating. Where soil is predominantly alkaline, acanthus, lilac, clematis and hawthorn are more likely to do well. Drought-resistant species such as broom, lavender, artemisia and rosemary indicate sandy soil, which dries out quickly. Flourishing annuals smothered with flowers – for example, nasturtiums and species of lychnis – are a sign of poor soil depleted of nutrients. Plants that can tolerate heavy clay include roses, lilac, forsythia and hellebores.

Preparing the Ground

The bare gardens of newly built houses, neglected vegetable patches or gardens reclaimed from the grip of brambles are all sites likely to benefit from rotavating once the site has been cleared of weeds.

Digging

Rotavators – motorized, hand-held tools like mini-ploughs which turn the earth over – are readily available to hire from lawnmower and garden machinery specialists. By using one, you'll be able to turn over the soil much faster than by digging, though the machine can be quite hard to handle until you get used to it.

All land must be dug from time to time. A fork or spade used to full depth turns over around 30 cm (1 ft) and aerates the soil, improving drainage and making root penetration easier. When cultivating an area for the first time, it can be a good idea to loosen the subsoil below the spade's depth by working a garden fork to and fro.

Digging is essential on heavy clay, where it can help to break down clods into a workable soil. Dig clay in the late autumn or early winter and let the weather help, too. Exploit the action of frost on large lumps of soil: it breaks them down into smaller and smaller pieces as water penetrates cracks in the clods, then freezes and forces them apart. Breaking up surface lumps with a rake helps this process.

Digging Wet Soil

Try to avoid digging soil when it is wet, as this is a surefire way to compact it. If you have to dig in less than ideal conditions, stand on a wooden board or plank to do it – by spreading your weight over a greater area, this lessens the chance of compaction.

Raised Beds for Flowering Plants

Where topsoil is particularly shallow, of poor quality or composed of heavy clay, you can create a good growing environment with a series of raised beds. In the flower garden, these can be permanent structures built from pressure-treated timber, logs, bricks or reclaimed railway sleepers.

Fill the structures with either bought-in topsoil or soil from elsewhere in the garden – for example, if you dig out a path or patio – and mix in plenty of well-rotted manure or general garden compost. Raised beds are an ideal way to bring flowers and small shrubs onto a bare terrace.

Customizing Soil

Use a raised bed to grow plants that otherwise wouldn't typically grow in your garden. Some of the most attractive plants that are fussy about soil type include camellias, rhododendrons and azaleas. These species absolutely refuse to grow in alkaline soil, but raised beds enable you to control the growing medium. By starting off with a mixture of special lime-free potting compost and manure or garden compost – both of which are acidic – you should be able to maintain the ideal environment for these species. Annual top dressings of leaf mould, pine needles or compost based on bracken or straw will help maintain acidity.

Compost

Making good compost is rather like following a healthy diet: too many rich ingredients and the compost heap starts to look distinctly unhealthy. Mix in some plain, 'high-fibre' elements and the end result is a pleasurable, sweet-smelling, crumbly compost.

What to include

Kitchen scraps make good compost. Keep a small tub by the sink and collect vegetable and fruit peelings, eggshells, used tea bags and coffee grounds. Grass clippings and weeds can be composted, but only add weeds pulled before they flower and set seed. New research has shown that newspaper, paper towels and tissues can be composted, as can thin cardboard like cereal boxes and toilet roll tubes. Crumple newspaper so that it aerates the compost heap rather than smothering it.

The key to perfect compost is to keep a balanced mixture, as too much of one ingredient can turn the heap into a slimy, foul-smelling mess.

Dealing with Weeds

Tenacious weeds such as bindweed (*Convolvulus arvensis*), couch grass (*Elymus repens*), creeping buttercup (*Ranunculus repens*) and ground elder (*Aegopodium podagraria*) can survive the composting process, especially if the heap doesn't get hot enough. To be absolutely certain that these weeds won't continue to wreak havoc in the borders, tie them up in a black plastic sack and leave them out in the sun for several weeks before composting.

What to Leave Out

Don't add meat, fish, bones, fats, oils or cooked scraps to the compost bin, as these are likely to attract rats and flies. Instead, invest in a wormery to deal with them. Too many twigs and leaves will delay the rotting process.

Compost Heaps and Containers

Composting can be as simple or as elaborate as you like. At its most basic you don't even need a container. Just start a heap on a patch of land that's not in use, using a base of twigs and branches to allow air to penetrate. Then one year later you can dig in the heap right where it's needed and cultivate that bed, meanwhile starting a new heap on a vacant bed.

In a small garden, a container will look neater. It is easy to make your own compost bin by recycling old materials. An old galvanized dustbin makes a neat composter. Knock the bottom out, punch some holes in the sides to allow air to circulate, and dig it into the ground a little to keep it stable. A plastic dustbin is just as good if you saw the bottom off and make similar air holes in the sides.

A wooden bin can be made by lashing together four wooden pallets or by nailing scrap timber to four posts firmly embedded in the earth. Using a pallet as a base for the heap improves air circulation, as does digging a cross-shaped trench and lining the sides so that they don't fall in.

Turning Over Old Leaves

Autumn leaves contain a tough protein called lignin, which is rotted down by fungi rather than bacteria, and the rotting process takes substantially longer than for other constituents of the compost heap. To avoid slowing the progress of the heap, make leaf mould separately. Sweep up the leaves and put them in black plastic rubbish sacks and tie the tops. Puncture the sacks with a garden fork and tuck them away in a corner for a year if possible. Or make a bin from a cylinder of chicken wire and wooden stakes, and cover with a scrap of old carpet to stop the leaves from blowing around. Some leaves rot more slowly than others – plane and chestnut, for example, are two of the slowest.

Manure

Introducing animal manure into soil adds nutrients and improves the soil's condition at the same time. Fresh manure can't be used directly, however, as it robs the soil of nitrogen when it rots down, starving plants of this vital nutrient and scorching leaves and roots. The main source of manure these days is horse manure, which can be converted to a well-rotted state in about six weeks. It needs to be stacked into a heap and firmed down by treading or flattening with a spade to remove air pockets. Cover the heap with plastic sheeting, weighted down all the way around, and let nature do the rest.

TREATING CHICKEN MANURE
Save the ash from a wood-burning stove or log fire and sprinkle it under the perches in the hen roost. The ash dries out the droppings and reduces the smell. At the same time a chemical reaction takes place between the ash and the droppings, resulting in a better-balanced manure than untreated chicken manure, which is so strong and high in nitrogen that it should not be used on its own. The wood ash and chicken manure mixture can be used directly on the soil.

Mulching

Covering the soil with a mulch – a thick layer that excludes the light – is a good way of reclaiming neglected land.

Old Carpets

To clear land effectively, scythe or rough-mow grass and weeds and rake them off the plot, then cover the area with the thickest, toughest old carpet you can find. Synthetic blends are best, as in extreme circumstances grass has been known to grow up through rotting wool-based carpets. To stop the carpets from blowing around, fix them to the ground with giant pins made by firmly hammering in bent wire coat-hangers. Put down the carpets in winter so that you have the whole year to make planting plans while the carpets put paid to couch grass and creeping buttercup. They will also trap plenty of emerging click beetles, whose larvae feed on plant roots and damage potatoes and carrots. Once land has been cleared in this way, it can be dug or rotavated and planted with potatoes to break up the soil.

Plastic Sheeting

For the ultimate no-weed vegetable bed, black plastic sheeting comes into its own. The sheeting is spread over the whole bed, and plants of the chosen crop are dug into the soil below it via cross-shaped slits in the sheeting. The one drawback is that it is virtually impossible to water the bed. The best way to get round this problem is to lay a leaky hose – either proper permeable tubing or a perforated garden hose – under the sheeting and attach it to the mains as needed. To keep the sheeting in position, dig the edges into trenches all the way around the bed.

Strawberries grow well using this method and the sheeting protects the berries from mud splashes. Potatoes can be planted through the cross-slits, too, and won't need earthing up, as the black plastic excludes the light.

Crop Rotation

Crop rotation is a traditional growing system based on moving crops around the land, in order to reduce the build-up of pests and diseases in the soil and to avoid depleting the soil of nutrients.

Four-times Table

The planting system is based on dividing vegetables into four groups: potatoes; peas and beans (legumes); the cabbage family (brassicas); and root crops. The vegetable plot is divided into four corresponding beds and each bed is planted with each crop in turn, on a four-yearly cycle. The crops have to be planted in a specific order for maximum benefit: one bed will be planted with potatoes in the first year, then with peas or beans in the second year, followed by cabbage of some type in the third year and finally with a root vegetable.

Potatoes do best in well-manured acid soil, as this reduces the likelihood of their developing potato scab. For the next crop – peas and beans – the soil will need liming to bring the pH back to neutral. Peas and beans are nitrogen-fixers, so when they are finished, the top growth should be cleared but the roots left to enrich the soil with nitrogen. In the third stage of the rotation the cabbages will be protected to some extent against club root disease by the previous year's lime – which is thought to be even more effective against the disease if it has been in the soil for a year or so. Finally come root crops: carrots, turnips, parsnips and onions.

In Strict Rotation

Potatoes cannot be planted straight after brassicas in crop rotation, as the lime that reduces club root disease in the cabbage family can promote potato scab. Always follow the strict rotation laid out on these pages to avoid this happening.

Sowing Direct

Sowing seed directly into the soil where plants are wanted is the easiest method, especially for vegetables and hardy annuals. The soil should be raked first to break down any large lumps, then raked again to the proverbial fine tilth before seed drills – shallow furrows – are marked out, using nothing more high-tech than a stick.

For best results, sow seed thinly. Most commercially available seed has good rates of germination, and if seeds are sown too thickly, seedlings will compete early on for light and water. Fine seed is the hardest to control: one tried and tested method is to mix 25 grams (1 oz) of seed with 250 millilitres (½ pint) of horticultural sand. Put the mixture in a bottle, insert a stopper made from a cork pierced with a drinking straw, then tip the bottle to sow the seed evenly.

Sowing Indoors

For an even earlier crop, sow seeds indoors or in a heated greenhouse, where they can be kept at a high temperature. Heating cables and mats are ideal for directing heat where it's needed. Seeds grown on a spare-bedroom window sill grow strongly towards the light so need turning daily; they should also be moved into the centre of the room at night, as the temperature close to the window falls dramatically. Never shut them between the curtains and the window, which is a recipe for certain failure.

A warm airing cupboard can be useful for germinating species that need high initial temperatures, but they need to be brought out the minute the seedlings emerge, as they will be weak and spindly if they spend time in the dark.

Taking Cuttings

For the small amount of effort involved in taking cuttings, the reward is a garden stocked with favourite shrubs, plants and flowers.

Easy Shrubs

The tree mallow (*Lavatera arborea*) is one of the easiest shrubs to propagate from cuttings, which seem to root no matter what time of year it is, though the traditional time to make cuttings of deciduous shrubs is autumn. Similar easily rooted species include elder (*Sambucus* – *S. nigra* is useful for native hedging), forsythia, willow (*Salix*), philadelphus and flowering currant (*Ribes*).

Cut stems about 25 cm (10 in) long, strip off any remaining leaves and cut off the growing tip just above a bud. Keep all cuttings where you can check their progress, in a prepared trench about 15 cm (6 in) deep with a layer of sand laid in the bottom to improve drainage. If you don't have a large garden, a trench can easily be squeezed in at the back of a border.

Propagating Roses

Roses are surprisingly easy to propagate from cuttings, and the big advantage of roses grown on their own roots is that you don't have to worry about suckers from the grafted rootstock overwhelming the plant. The main reason that nurseries sell roses on grafted rootstocks is speed – they produce saleable plants a lot more quickly than cuttings. But since commercial considerations don't come into amateur gardening, rose cuttings are well worth taking. In autumn, take cuttings of stems that are about a year old, roughly the thickness of a pencil and about 15 cm (6 in) long. Trim them back to a bud at each end, then just push them into the soil in a sheltered corner and wait. In a year's time they should be strong enough to transplant into their final growing positions.

Pots and Seed Trays

Every gardener needs a range of plant pots. Nothing can beat terracotta for sheer good looks, but it does have some disadvantages. Terracotta is porous, which means the soil within dries out faster and plants need more frequent watering than their counterparts in plastic containers. Large pots are extremely heavy when planted up, and, whatever their size, terracotta pots are easily broken.

Ageing Terracotta

There are several tried and tested methods for ageing new terracotta. Painting pots with yogurt or liquid manure encourages algae and moss growth. Rubbing new pots with parsley turns them instantly green, mimicking algal bloom, but the process is wearing on the fingertips and very fiddly. Faking age with artists' pigment paints is quickest: mix different earthy tones with a water-resistant glue and sponge them onto your pots for instant antiquity.

Storing Pots

Any terracotta pots that aren't permanently planted up should be stored in a shed for the winter. Scrub them well and leave them to dry first. Small pots can be laid on their sides, tucked loosely inside each other, in a strong wooden tray. Never store pots in upright stacks, as changes in temperature and humidity can cause them to swell and stick tightly together, resulting in inevitable breakages as you try to prise them apart.

The Pros and Cons of Plastic

Terracotta's porosity gives it a tendency to harbour plant diseases, whereas plastic pots are easy to sterilize: simply wash them in a very weak bleach solution and leave them to dry. Plastic pots are very cheap to buy, but there is a limit to the number you can re-use for seedlings and as gifts for neighbours, so they are also wasteful.

Choice of Containers

As well as conventional plastic and terracotta pots, look out for household objects that have outgrown their usefulness but could be reinvented as planters.

Old-fashioned tin baby-baths look wonderful massed with petunias, and clay chimney pots are ideal for trailing campanulas, verbenas or petunias. Anyone who has spent a holiday in Greece can't fail to have noticed the empty cooking-oil drums –

either painted or left boldly in their original state – that have been recycled to hold geraniums and lilies.

What any unconventional container must have is drainage: a hand drill can come in handy to pierce metal tins, while a nail heated in a gas flame should be sufficient to melt holes in plastic. Raising containers slightly off the ground on bricks, battens or staging will help prevent drainage holes from becoming blocked.

What to Plant

Containers offer a lot more scope for colour and interest through seasonal planting – filling pots in summer with colourful annuals and replanting them with pansies or heather for winter colour, underplanted with spring bulbs for the following season.

Permanent plantings tend to get rather neglected and tired-looking as the potting compost becomes exhausted of nutrients. Having said that, with proper attention, some shrubs can be grown permanently in containers and can actually benefit from having their roots restricted, promoting extra flowers in compensation. Species of rhododendrons, camellias and pieris can all be

pot-grown, so long as they are top-dressed with well-rotted manure in spring.

Hanging Baskets

Hanging baskets are notoriously vulnerable to drying out, so you must be rigorous about watering in hot weather. A good liner will help reduce water loss.

Traditionally, wire baskets were lined with moss or foam, but you can now buy liners fabricated from recycled wool, from coconut fibre and from card, all of which come in unobtrusive sludgy colours. In addition, an old saucer placed at the bottom of the liner before you add the compost will act as a shallow reservoir when you water the basket.

To be successful, hanging baskets need to look good from every angle – and that includes from underneath. To add plants all the way around the basket, carefully push their roots through the mesh or bars of the basket.

Window Boxes

Well-maintained window boxes can transform the façade of a house, but, conversely, nothing looks sadder than a few desiccated stalks in a neglected planter.

Proportions are important, too: make or buy a window box that is the full length of the window sill – boxes that are too small look silly. Keep plantings low so that you don't obscure the light in the room and also so that you can open the window easily to water and feed flowers. The window box will need drainage holes in the base, and also a drainage layer. If the window box is heavy, fix it to the walls of the window recess with L-shaped galvanized brackets – you don't want to risk injuring visitors or passers-by.

Weed Control

Before you plan a strategy for dealing with weeds, first ask yourself, what is a weed? All gardeners need their own personal definitions.

In a wild garden or an informal cottage border, many so-called weeds that are actually wildflowers can look charming mixed in with cultivated species. Herb Robert (*Geranium robertianum*), for example, is a delicate cousin of hardy geraniums, with red-stemmed leaves and pretty pink flowers.

Red campion (*Silene dioica*) is related to the showier annual lychnis species and is a welcome plant in shady spots; while statuesque teasels make ideal back-of-border plants. Late in the year, ivy is a valuable source of nectar for bees, and provides cover for roosting birds and nesting sites in spring. Don't be in a hurry to pull up nettles, either – they are a caterpillar food plant and also a lifeline for ladybirds, which rely on nettle aphids as a food source early in the year.

Cunning Weeds

Then there are weeds that try to fool you by looking pretty. Don't be weak and let creeping buttercup (*Ranunculus repens*) stay because its flowers contrast nicely with a purple hardy geranium: you'll regret it. More deceptively pretty thugs include ground ivy (*Glechoma hederacea*) and cinquefoil (*Potentilla reptans*) – pull them up on sight. Some weeds appear aggravatingly like proper plants: until it flowers, wood avens (*Geum urbanum*) looks just like rosettes of its cultivated relative geum, and it can take over a border in an instant.

Pernicious weeds

The hardest weeds to eradicate are bindweed (*Convolvulus arvensis*), ground elder (*Aegopodium podagraria*), couch grass (*Elymus repens*) and creeping thistle (*Cirsium arvense*).

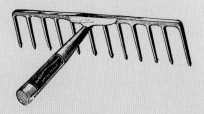

Pruning

Pruning can improve a plant's shape and appearance, encourage more flowers or fruit and keep the size of shrubs and trees in check.

Tools are crucial to pruning. Secateurs (pruning shears) are fine for use on woody shrubs but are generally designed to cope with fairly narrow stems – about 1 cm (⅜ in) in diameter. For bigger stems, a pruning saw or long-handled pruners are more efficient. Blunt blades or inadequate tools will crush stems rather than slicing cleanly, making wood vulnerable to pests and infection.

Roses

Much of the pruning lore attached to roses is a legacy of the Victorian mania for producing prize blooms for exhibition, without too much thought for the appearance of the bush in the garden. All you really need to do is regularly remove the dead flower heads from repeat-flowering varieties, in order to keep a good flush of flowers going, and prune in spring in order to encourage vigorous growth, cutting back weak, spindly shoots hardest of all. Trials have shown little difference between roses pruned to a careful regime and those lightly sheared with hedge clippers.

Gradual Pruning

When restoring a neglected garden, don't be in too much of a hurry to hack back overgrown roses. Cutting an ancient rose right back in one go could prove such a shock to its system that the plant could die. Instead, exercise patience and cut it back by about one-third of its growth each year to rejuvenate it with lots of healthy new shoots.

Shrubs

The general rule when pruning shrubs is to note when the species flowers. Shrubs that flower after midsummer should be trimmed back in early spring, while spring-flowering shrubs are best pruned straight after they have flowered, to boost next year's blooms. Buds always grow in the direction in which they are pointing, so for a balanced shape, trim above an outward-facing bud. Cutting too close to the bud risks damaging it, but, equally, leaving too long a stub causes unsightly dieback above it. By making the cut at an angle so that rainwater runs off, the stem is less likely either to rot or become infected.

Hedges

One of the most important considerations when pruning a hedge is to wait until the nesting season is over, to avoid disturbing garden birds. For a clipped formal boundary, trim bushes into a wedge shape, wider at the bottom than the top. This allows rain and sun to reach all parts of the hedge equally. Evergreen hedges must be well maintained from the very start, as you cannot cut into old wood – it simply won't regrow.

Pest Control

Slugs are a near-universal garden problem. Methods of trapping them rely on their habit of hiding during the day: setting out grapefruit halves or slabs of wood and turning them over every morning usually reveals a fair number of slugs. If you can bear it, leave the traps upturned and wait for the birds to deal with them. They make a welcome snack for any nearby ducks or can be thrown into a pond for the fish to find.

Creating barriers is another traditional method used to deter slug attack. Rings of soot, crushed eggshells, pine needles, ash and slaked lime sprinkled around vulnerable young plants are known to deter slugs with varying degrees of success. A more modern trick is to cut the bottom off a clear plastic drinks bottle and use this as a mini-cloche to protect a small plant. These remedies apply to snails, too.

SLUGS AND SNAILS
Slugs and snails are almost unstoppable and are one reason why it makes sense to grow more vegetables than you think you're going to need. Here they've eaten a ruby chard leaf down to the tough midrib.

Lawns

There's no getting away from it, lawns are the most labour-intensive area of the garden – that is, if you want a weed-free velvet sward rather than daisy-starred turf.

Lawnmowers were invented in the 1830s; before then, the grass was scythed then rolled to smooth out any ragged patches where the turf had been torn up. Once the lawnmower became commonplace, mechanized leaf-sweepers, edging shears and all manner of paraphernalia that is still familiar today soon followed.

Starting From Scratch

The quickest way to create a lawn is to lay turves, but as these are expensive, sowing a lawn is still a good option if you have the time. The traditional time to sow is late summer, but early spring is a good second best. The ground needs to be dug shallowly, then firmed and raked to an even tilth before seed is scattered and raked in.

Fine-leaved Festuca and Agrostis species make a beautiful lawn but are not hard-wearing enough for family use; mixtures of ryegrass (*Lolium perenne*) and meadow grass (*Poa* spp.) are the toughest. For the most fragrant lawn try to get hold of seed for sweet vernal grass (*Anthoxanthum odoratum*) and mix some in – it contains coumarin for that characteristic new-mown hay smell.

Keep sparrows off a newly sown area by swathing it in horticultural fleece or, more traditionally, stringing it with black cotton, which deters birds from landing there.

Dealing with Dandelions

To get rid of rosette-forming weeds on a lawn – dandelion, plantain, daisy – carefully tip a teaspoon of salt into the centre of each cluster of leaves. This will kill the plant. If there aren't too many plants, just cut them out with a pocket knife and fill any resulting gap with a little potting compost.

The Cutting Garden

Preparing and Planting

While the ground should be cleared of weeds, it's not necessary to manure it heavily, as rich soil can produce lush growth at the expense of flowers. For spring bouquets, plant as many  daffodils and tulips as you can cram in; you can safely ignore the recommended spacing distances as you are not making a permanent planting. Plant them in neat blocks, and criss-cross the cutting garden with plank paths so that you can reach the flowers easily when you need to cut them.

Cottage garden annuals are easy to raise from seed, and they make charming summer posies. Try clarkia, godetia, love-in-a-mist (*Nigella damascena*), cosmos, larkspur (*Consolida ambigua*) and sweet scabious (*Scabiosa atropurpurea*). For tall arrangements, grow hollyhocks, bells of Ireland (*Moluccella laevis*) with its curious green flowers, *Verbena bonariensis*, which has an open airy shape and small purple flowers, and the exotic-looking spider flower (*Cleome spinosa*), which is easily raised from seed. A plot of just 10 x 15 ft will be large enough.

When to Cut

Always cut flowers in the early morning, when moisture and sugar content are high. Take a bucket of water with you into the garden and immerse the stems as soon as they are cut. When you are ready to arrange the flowers, recut them underwater to avoid getting an airlock in the stems that would slow down water uptake.

air

Predicting the Weather

Although the latest technology means that meteorologists are able to bring us detailed forecasts and long-range predictions, weather patterns still vary locally. By keeping a note of cold spells and by talking to nursery growers and other gardeners in your neighbourhood, it's possible to build up a personalized weather map that will help you take the best possible advantage of the local climate.

A Cold Snap

Unseasonable frost is one of a gardener's worst enemies. A cold, starry night, when there's no wind and no dew on the grass, is a pretty sure indication that the temperature is going to drop below freezing. Gardeners in the milder south should watch out for northerly winds bringing cold weather; in the north, clear weather following wind or rain can herald a sharp drop in temperature. Snow is less of a problem since, once in place, it forms an insulating blanket across plants. It is often heralded by a curious grey tone to the sky from diffuse cirrus-type ice clouds, accompanied by a halo around the sun or moon.

Snow and Ice

Knock thick snow from evergreen trees and shrubs, to stop the weight of the snow from breaking or permanently bending branches. Don't do the same for heavy ice, however. Let it thaw gradually or you risk breaking the branches.

Frost

Frost can be beautiful as well as treacherous, etching winter stems and seedheads with ice crystals. Don't be in too much of a hurry to tidy up the garden or you won't be able to see pretty effects – and the dead material offers a degree of protection to the dormant plant below.

Frost Protection

Preparing for Late Frosts

Late spring frosts can put paid to a whole season of flowers, but if you know low temperatures are imminent, there are a few rescue operations. An old sheet thrown over a hydrangea bush or small magnolia will protect its flower buds – use clothes pegs to fasten it to twiggy branches. Use a cloth that reaches to the ground, as the object is to trap radiant heat from the earth and keep the temperature under the cloth above freezing point. Use the same principle to protect beds of smaller delicate species. Horticultural fleece is very efficient, but plastic sheeting or newspaper will do the trick – whichever you use, weight down the edges with bricks or stones.

The roots of container-grown plants are vulnerable to freezing, and it is a sensible precaution to wrap pots in layers of sacking, newspaper or bubble wrap. It may not look very attractive but neither does a dead plant. To protect the plant itself, make cones or teepees of newspaper stapled in place.

Homemade Mini-Heaters

To keep a cold greenhouse or conservatory frost-free, make your own candle lamps. Stand a candle in a terracotta pot, using a layer of sand in the bottom for extra stability. Then light the candle and invert a pot of the same size over it, to form a safe mini-heater that will take the chill off the air – you'll need several to make a difference, perhaps more, depending on the size of the greenhouse.

Windbreaks

A windbreak can go a long way, quite literally, towards reducing the scorching effects of strong winds.

Slowing Down

What is needed is something to slow the wind down rather than stop it. Solid walls or fences cause more problems than they prevent: when the wind hits the barrier it actually increases in speed as it rushes over the top and whirls and eddies on the theoretically sheltered side. A permeable barrier that filters and slows strong gusts will protect delicate plants more effectively.

Trellis makes a useful windbreak, provided it is strongly anchored. Using a green woodstain will make it less conspicuous, and climbing plants can be trained up it for both ornamental effect and added shelter. Similarly, chainmail fencing makes a good windbreak and, though rather ugly on its own, is easily disguised with creepers and climbers.

Hedges are the best windbreaks but they do have drawbacks. They will compete for water and nutrients with the plants they shelter, and they can take up a great deal of room.

Preventing Frost Pockets

Creating a windbreak by planting a hedge or building a fence across sloping land can actually trap cold air in a garden and turn it into a frost pocket. To prevent this from happening, clear out the bottom of the hedge regularly so that air can flow in and out. Leave a gap at the base of a fence for a similar air flow.

Greenhouses

Wood or Metal?

A wooden-framed greenhouse will usually look better than an aluminium-framed version, particularly in a traditional garden setting, but will need more maintenance. Softwood greenhouses need painting regularly to stop the wood from rotting – creosoting the wood to preserve it is not an option as it produces fumes toxic to plants.

Hardwood frames are far more weather-resistant but more expensive.

Whether you choose a traditional rectangular greenhouse or a lean-to against the house, you must make sure your model has adequate ventilation to control temperature and humidity in summer, plus shading of some kind to prevent fierce sunlight from scorching plants.

To Heat or Not?

A fully heated greenhouse will support exotic species, but at a price. For the average garden, cheaper options include simply keeping the greenhouse frost-free, by using a small paraffin heater or even a thermostatically controlled electric heater that kicks in when the temperature drops.

A frost-free greenhouse is ideal for overwintering tender fuchsias and pelargoniums and for starting off the more unusual species of spring and summer bulbs. Rather than heat the air, electric cables can be laid to heat the soil in the beds, or in trays on the staging if you want to give seedlings a helpful boost.

Making a Hot Bed

Traditional kitchen gardens that served great country houses of the past had elaborate hot beds for raising exotic fruits like pineapples and melons for the table. The same principle can be used in the greenhouse on a more modest scale to grow cucumbers, aubergines (eggplants) and melons.

To make a hot bed, you need fresh – not well-rotted, for once – strawy horse manure. Make a thick layer on the greenhouse border and cover it with a thin sprinkling of soil and a dusting of lime. Repeat the process two more times, then dig planting holes in the hot bed and fill them with potting compost. Add the plants of your choice and cover all with a final layer of soil. As the manure rots down it heats up and warms the plants gently – a great boon for slightly fussy crops.

Biological Warfare

Deal with greenhouse infestations of whitefly with the newest method – biological control. Various companies can supply parasitic wasps, which are sent in egg form by mail order. *Encarsia formosa* lays its eggs in the bodies of whitefly, and the developing larvae kill off the host. Similar biological predators exist for other pests, including red spider mite, vine weevils, aphids and scale insects. Biological control tends to work best in the enclosed environment of a greenhouse, where the insects are in close contact with their prey.

Scented Flowers

Roses have one of the sweetest scents, especially the old garden roses that flower for just a few short weeks each summer. Blowsy full-blown cabbage roses (*Rosa x centifolia)* have the most intoxicating scent of all – 'Fantin-Latour' is a perfect example with its many-petalled flowers in palest pink. The best way to appreciate roses is to train a climbing variety or two over an arch that encloses a bench. 'Gloire de Dijon' and 'Zéphirine Drouhin' are two headily perfumed climbing roses that will soon embrace a simple arch, turning it into a fragrant bower in which to sit and dream. The vigorous rambling rose 'Albertine' has bright pink flowers that fade gracefully to blush pink as they age and a wonderfully fruity, lemony perfume.

SWEET PEAS

To keep sweet peas flowering right through the summer, never let them set seed. As soon as seed pods begin to swell, the plant quite rightly feels its job is done and produces fewer and fewer flowers. At the same time, keep the plants well watered, especially in dry weather.

Scented Pathways

Planting a pathway with aromatic herbs makes walking around the garden doubly pleasant.

Cushions of thyme spilling over from the border release a pungent scent when bruised by passing feet, while lemon verbena grows tall enough to be brushed and crushed with the hand as you pass. Marjoram, santolina and sage make suitably fragrant edge-of-path plants, while rosemary and lavender bushes planted under the washing line are a lovely way to perfume clothes and bed linen.

Garden seats are another prime site for perfumed plants. If you don't have a rose bower to sit in, you can make an equally fragrant spot by planting sweet rocket (*Hesperis matronalis*) and sweet mignonette (*Reseda lutea*) beside a bench. Growing lilies in pots that can be moved near garden seats or onto a terrace allows their beauty and fragrance to be fully appreciated as a succession of blooms wax and wane.

Scented pelargoniums are vastly underrated. Their elegantly shaped leaves release a surprising variety of scents when crushed. The best known is the lemon geranium, but their perfumes range from mint chocolate to orange, and from an aromatic resinous scent to a hint of rose like the fragrance of Turkish delight.

Early Fragrance

Cut a stem of wintersweet (*Chimonanthus spp.*) while the flowers are still in bud and bring it indoors for forcing. The warmth will induce it to bloom early and its honeyed scent will perfume a room for days. Try the same technique with mahonia, witch hazel (*Hamamelis spp.*) and clove-scented *Daphne mezereum* or *D. odora*.

Seeds

Self-Seeding

Letting plants self-seed saves a fair amount of work in the garden and a little expense too. If you don't like the position in which a plant has seeded itself, you can in most cases shift it somewhere more suitable, but some fortuitous, unplanned combinations can occur in this way. Plants to let have their head include forget-me-nots (*Myosotis*), love-in-a-mist (*Nigella damascena*), lychnis (*Lychnis coronaria*), foxgloves (*Digitalis purpurea*), sweet rocket (*Hesperis matronalis*), honesty (*Lunaria annua*), hellebores, aquilegias and some campanulas. Once introduced into a garden, these prolific self-seeders are likely to stay if they find conditions to their liking.

Collecting Seed

If you prefer to have more control over the siting of plants, it is worth collecting seed and storing it for sowing the following year. It's best to leave seedheads to ripen on the plant and cut them just before the seed is released. In practice, this takes quite a bit of judgement and it can be easier to cut the whole stem, tie paper bags over the seedheads and hang them up in a dry, airy room or shed. Never use plastic bags: they retain moisture and lead to rotting or mould developing.

You can collect seed from anything you like, but only seed from actual species or long-established cultivars will come 'true', that is, resemble the parent plant. However, it can be quite exciting to sow collected delphinium seed, for example, and see what dazzling flowers it throws up.

Plants for Sun

Growing plants in a sunny garden is easy: there's no need to give too much thought to what you can and cannot grow. Making a similar display in a shady garden, however, requires more planning and artifice.

With a shady garden there are plants that you must forget about – to hanker after them is useless. In a sunny garden there are very few plants that will not grow, especially as it is easy to create a shady spot somewhere. There are disadvantages to a totally sunny site, though, such as the fact that you have to water plants more frequently. Also, if the garden is hot and dry, it may be too sunny for typical herbaceous sun lovers, and so you may have to restrict your planting to drought-tolerant species.

Sun Lovers

Most of the great stalwarts of the herbaceous border need full sun to produce the best blooms. Delphiniums grown in a shady site, for example, will flower but the flower spikes will be sparsely scattered with individual florets instead of densely packed. Overall growth will be weak and spindly, too. It's implicit from their name that sunflowers must be grown in an open sunny site so that their huge heads can follow the sun's path across the sky.

The Vegetable Garden

There's no compromise between sun and shade when growing food crops. Vegetables, soft fruit and tree fruits all depend on the sun to ripen them, and the vegetable plot should be sited in the sunniest part of the garden.

Plants in Shade

The most obvious option to adopt when planting up a shady site is to create a woodland garden. In this way you can take maximum advantage of early spring light when trees and shrubs are only just coming into leaf.

Spring bulbs and tubers such as bluebells (*Hyacinthoides non-scripta*), snowdrops (*Galanthus spp.*), wood anemones (*Anemone nemorosa*), crocuses and dog's-tooth violets (*Erythronium dens-canis*) will all flourish under the open canopy of trees and shrubs and sink back into obscurity as the shade thickens later in the year.

Dry Shade

The worst possible gardening conundrum is dry shade. Thankfully, few gardens are completely dry and shady, but most have an awkward spot where precious few plants will grow – even weeds. The solution is to grow ferns, such as evergreen species of asplenium and *Polypodium vulgare*, which are at home in dry shade. Ferns will need a little help to get established, with copious watering and some well-rotted manure forked into the soil. But once they are strong enough, they can cope with the most unpromising situations and actually beautify them.

Shrubs for Dappled Shade

Hydrangeas are perfect shrubs for dappled shade – their native habitat is the edge of woodland in

Japan. They bring colour to a shady garden at a traditionally 'dead' time of year – many species come into bloom in late summer and continue until the first frosts. There are three main flower types to choose from: classic mopheads; lace caps; and panicles, which have long loose flowers rather like sprays of lilac.

Drying Flowers

Dried flowers are big business and shop-bought arrangements are not cheap. By setting aside a row or two in the cutting garden or the vegetable plot, you can dry your own flowers and create year-round displays very easily.

What to Grow

The easiest flowers to dry are those specifically grown for that purpose – the so-called 'everlasting flowers' or 'immortelles'. Strawflowers (*Helichrysum bracteatum*) are like stiff-petalled daisies in hot shades of scarlet, gold and yellow, and *Xeranthemum annuum* has purple, pink or white flowers and attractive woolly leaves.

Whether fresh or dried, gypsophila (baby's breath) is a useful flower for filling in spaces in any arrangement. The familiar colourful statice (*Limonium*), also known as sea lavender, tolerates dry conditions and extreme heat – even salt spray – making it useful in the garden as well as for drying. Ornamental grasses dry well. Look out for evocatively named quaking grass (*Briza spp*.), with its purplish-brown spikelets dangling from thin stalks; hare's-tail grass (*Lagurus ovatus*), which has fluffy flower heads resembling, as its name suggests, hares' tails; and foxtail millet (*Setaria italica*), with its densely packed flower heads.

How to Dry

All the species listed above can simply be cut and hung upside down in bunches in a warm dark cupboard or attic

for two to three weeks. Some other garden flowers also respond successfully to this simple treatment, including larkspur (*Consolida*), love-in-a-mist (*Nigella damascena*), globe thistle (*Echinops*) and goldenrod (*Solidago spp*.).

Attractive seedheads can be cut straight from the garden and may not need further drying, but if they do, hang them in a large paper carrier bag or they'll scatter seed everywhere.

Storing Fruit

Storing Apples

To keep a supply of apples throughout the winter you need to start by growing late-ripening varieties. Pick them in late autumn or early winter when they are fully ripe. Use a cloth-lined basket to avoid bruising the apples as you gather them, then pick over the apples carefully and store only the best. Apples can be stored on trays, arranged so that the fruits don't touch each other, or wrapped individually to slow the spread of mould or rot.

One old method advocates lining trays or crates with dried elderflowers before adding the apples. This is said to prolong storage and also to give the apples a distinctive hint of pineapple. A more modern method is to pack fruit in plastic bags, sealed with a twist of wire but perforated with pinpricks so that the fruit can 'breathe'. Whichever method you choose, check regularly for rot or disease and remove any rotten fruit.

Drying Apples

There are various ways of drying apples, involving either heat or air. To dry them in a very slow oven – the warming oven of an Aga or Rayburn is ideal – first peel and core the apples and soak them in salted water. Slice them thickly, then pat them dry before laying the slices on metal cake-cooling racks. In a conventional oven, dry them on the lowest setting with the door ajar. Do this for three to four hours a day, for up to four days. When the slices are completely hard they should be left out in the air for a couple more days before being stored in an airtight container.

Alternatively, you can simply slice peeled and cored apples, thread the slices on string and hang the resulting necklaces above a radiator for up to a week. The slices will shrink but won't harden – they'll just feel leathery. Then pack them in plastic bags.

Storing Vegetables

Savoy cabbages can stay in the ground all winter long but less robust varieties can be pulled and stored by hanging them upside down – root and stalk still attached – in a dry, frost-free shed, alongside strings of garlic and onions. They'll keep in this way for around two months.

Potatoes are best stored in a frost-free shed. Use only permeable hessian (burlap) or paper sacks and pack them with top-quality specimens. Every six weeks, carefully tip out the contents and sort through them, removing any potatoes that show signs of rot or deterioration.

Other root crops can be stored in old-fashioned peat boxes, though in these conservation-conscious times, it is better to use horticultural sand or vermiculite than peat. Carrots should have their tops cut off after lifting and then be laid on a bed of sand in a wooden box with no roots touching. Cover them with sand and add more layers until the box is full.

Stringing Onions

To string up onions for storage, start with a length of string and a single onion. Double over the string and fasten to the onion stalk with a simple slip knot.

Leave the onion hanging from the double strand of string and add more as follows. Take the next onion and, holding the stalk, thread the onion between the two strings. Wrap it around both strings and then bring it back through the middle of the two. Its own weight will help to keep the stalk in position. Build up the onion string by repeating the process.

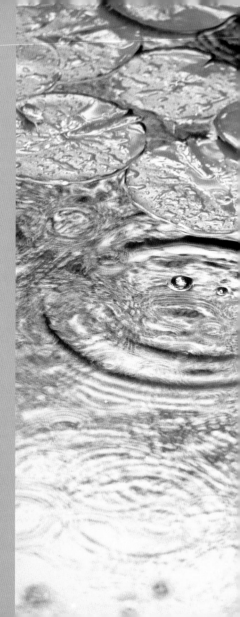

water

Collecting Water

Increasingly, water is valued as a precious resource, so it makes sense to collect, conserve and recycle water in any way possible.

A water butt collects rainwater via the downpipe (downspout) that channels rain from the gutter into the drain or soakaway. With an average-sized roof, you should be able to install several

butts at strategic points around the exterior of the house. Even a garage, shed or greenhouse with a pitched roof yields a useful amount of rainwater.

Keeping a lid on a butt is important to stop small animals – not to mention children – from falling in. It also deters mosquitoes from breeding in the water (the larval stage in their life cycle takes place underwater).

Watering Cans

The plastic versus metal debate comes into consideration when choosing a watering can. There's no doubt that plastic is lighter and easier to carry, but it doesn't age well and will split and crack when subjected to extremes of temperature. Galvanized metal, on the other hand, gains character as the years go by, becoming as treasured as a favourite pair of boots or a battered old hat.

Never leave metal watering cans outside in winter. Any rain that collects inside will freeze on a frosty night and the expanding ice will buckle the base, making the can wobbly and unusable.

The most useful size of watering can is about 9 litres (2 gallons). A watering can with a detachable rose is best – provided you are rigorous about returning it to the same shelf in the shed after use.

Lime-Free Water

An extra benefit of collecting rainwater in hard-water areas is that it is ideal for watering lime-hating shrubs like camellias and rhododendrons. If you've already grown them in lime-free compost, rainwater won't undo your effort.

The Best Time of Day

If possible, avoid watering in full sunshine on a hot day. Any water droplets that splash onto a plant's leaves will act as mini-magnifying glasses, focusing the sun's rays and scorching the leaves. Watering at the hottest time of the day also increases the humidity in the area immediately around the plant, producing ideal conditions for fungal spores of diseases such as powdery mildew and grey mould to germinate and multiply.

The cool of the evening has always been the traditional time to water plants, whether in the garden or in pots, as water is less likely to evaporate and has more chance of being taken up by roots. But recent studies have indicated that these very conditions, while benefiting plants, also encourage slugs and snails to come and browse, whereas seedlings watered at the beginning of the day suffer less damage. It's certainly worth experimenting with early-morning watering, even if it is only when plants are small and less able to withstand the onslaught of slugs and snails.

Watering Techniques

When watering a plant, it is all too easy to wash away the surface soil and leave delicate roots exposed, especially if you are using a hose or a full watering can. When you are digging-in new plants, prepare in advance and reduce the risk of this happening by firming the soil at the base of the plant into a shallow depression. When you water, this 'basin' will hold the water close to the plant, letting it seep down to the roots gradually and stopping any soil from being washed away.

It is best to give a plant a thorough soaking just once a week rather than a quick sprinkling more frequently.

Insufficient watering encourages roots to grow shallowly as the water doesn't penetrate to any great depth, causing the plant more stress as the roots are likely to be exposed or uprooted in strong wind.

Watering Plants in Pots

On a hot summer's day, when container-grown plants may need watering twice daily, the practicality of plastic pots can outweigh terracotta's good looks. Plastic at least has the virtue of retaining some water, whereas moisture evaporates quickly from terracotta. In a really hot spell, it may be worth shifting pots to a shadier spot to sit out the heatwave.

When planting up containers earlier in the year, consider using water-retaining granules. A real scientific breakthrough, these long-chain polyacrylamides can hold many times their weight in water, which then becomes available to plants as the potting compost dries out. The granules can be either added to potting compost and watered thoroughly, or stirred in a bucket of water until they have swollen and then mixed into the compost.

Watering Lawns

An established lawn should be tough enough to recover from lack of rain, but a newly sown or laid patch may need watering in its first year or two. A sprinkler is the best way to do it – move it around as each area becomes soaked. To make sure water penetrates to the grass roots on compacted soil, spike the lawn with a garden fork.

Water Cure

If a plant that has finished flowering is looking tatty – its leaves scorched and damaged, even mildewed – cut it right back to ground level and give it a thorough soaking with at least one full watering can. Within a matter of weeks, it will have put out fresh new growth and will be a worthy member of the border again.

Irrigation

While it may be galling to watch flowering perennials fail to thrive during a scorching summer, they may at least do better the following year. But in the vegetable garden you get only one chance, so it makes sense to plan some kind of standby irrigation system to compensate for lack of rain.

Lengths of plastic guttering, pierced at intervals and laid between rows of carrots, potatoes or beans, will direct water far more efficiently than a watering can. Just empty the watering can at the top of the gutter and let gravity do the rest.

Leaking Pipes

Some manufacturers have produced irrigation systems based on porous piping, which can be either buried permanently in the soil or laid along the surface, and connected to an outside tap (faucet) when needed. You can make a somewhat crude version yourself by sabotaging an old garden hose and making small cuts along its length with a sharp knife. Lay the hose up and down the rows of vegetables and firmly plug the open end with a stopper, then turn the tap on carefully and slowly.

Capillary Systems

Rudimentary irrigation systems can be useful in a greenhouse or for a collection of planted containers. To keep greenhouse plants watered, line plastic trays with capillary matting and stand groups of pots on top. Then use narrow strips of the capillary matting or lengths of twine or string (not nylon-based) to link the trays to a container of water: these will act as wicks and allow the plants to draw moisture from the matting and reservoir. This method is very useful for keeping house plants alive and happy while you are away from the garden on holiday.

Mulching to Retain Moisture

A mulch – a layer of manure, compost, bark chippings or other material used as a top dressing – not only improves soil and suppresses weeds (see page 32), but can also be used as a barrier to stop evaporation and keep the earth moist.

Mulching for water conservation can only be done after a good downpour, however – anything less and you will simply add to the water problem, by preventing subsequent rainfall from penetrating the mulch and reaching the plants. By the same token, if you improve the water-retaining properties of the soil itself by manuring when you are preparing the earth you will be giving flower and vegetable beds a head start, which you can then build on by mulching.

Applying Mulch

For a layer of well-rotted manure to be effective at reducing evaporation, it needs to be 5 to 7.5 cm (2 to 3 in) deep. Leave a clear margin around each plant so that the mulch doesn't touch stem or leaves, which would cause them to rot. Eventually the mulch will be broken down by rain and by worm action, but it will at least last longer than if it had been forked into the soil.

Grass cuttings can make a useful mulch but they are tricky to use. If you spread them too thinly, they won't do the job properly, but if you layer them too thickly, so that the air is excluded, they may form an unpleasant-smelling slime.

To Keep Grass Green

During very dry spells, take the hood off the lawn mower and let the grass cuttings lie where they fall on the lawn. They will act as a mulch and help to keep the grass looking greener for longer.

Making Your Own Fertilizers

Readymade liquid fertilizers are concentrated and convenient. Based on animal manure or on seaweed extracts, they should be diluted according to the manufacturer's instructions. But if you have the time and the inclination, it's very easy to make your own liquid manure.

Just half-fill an old hessian (burlap) sack with well-rotted manure – any sort will do – and tie the top tightly. Then lower the sack into a large drum of water or even into a water butt, leaving a length of string showing so you can haul the sack out after two or three weeks when the water has turned as dark as mahogany (the sack will be very heavy by then so you may need assistance). Provided the soil isn't dry, you can use this liquid to water plants directly, or you can dilute it with an equal amount of water and use it as a foliar feed.

High-Potash Feed ·

The perennial plant comfrey is rich in potash, an essential nutrient for flowering and fruit formation. To make a high-potash feed, fill an old plastic bowl with comfrey leaves and cover the leaves with water. Put a piece of old board across the bowl for a lid and leave for several weeks, stirring it from time to time. When the leaves have rotted, strain off the liquid and dilute it by ten parts of water to one of liquid before using it on the borders or vegetable patch. The leaf debris can go on the compost heap. This method also works well with nettles, which you can gather from the hedgerows.

Ponds

Not only are ponds stylishly ornamental – opening up a garden by mirroring the sky and creating a perfect spot for tranquil reflection – but they also encourage wildlife into the garden, with great benefits for plants and gardener. No garden is too small for a pond. Even a half barrel sunk to its rim in the soil, or simply placed on a patio, filled with water and planted with a single water lily, qualifies as an honorary pond or water feature, and it will still attract dragonflies and birds at the very least.

A larger pond will entice frogs and toads – both valuable allies in the war against slugs and snails – into the garden and they may even breed. It will also be a source of drinking water for small mammals like hedgehogs, similarly important consumers of slugs and snails.

WATER LILIES
Water lily leaves float on the surface off a pond, but if the plant becomes congested, the leaves actually grow up above the surface to gain more space.

Water-Loving Plants

Plants for the Water's Edge

Plants that thrive right at the water's edge include arum lilies (*Zantedeschia aethiopica*), yellow skunk cabbage (*Lysichiton americanus*) and the pickerel weed (*Pontederia cordata*) with its spires of blue summer flowers; these all love having their roots in the warm shallows. For a more natural look, add various native species like brooklime (*Veronica beccabunga*), figwort (*Scrophularia auriculata*), marsh marigolds (*Caltha palustris*) and wild irises (*Iris versicolor* and *I. pseudacorus*, blue and yellow respectively).

Deep-Water Plants

Although deep-water plants like water lilies produce floating leaves and flowers, their roots must be firmly anchored. Start by planting water lilies in special perforated pots or baskets, lined with sacking or hessian (burlap) to stop the soil from washing away – use specially prepared 'aquatic soil' rather than economizing with garden soil, which can upset the nutrient balance of the pond. Add a layer of gravel to prevent the soil from floating out when you submerge the pot, then gently place the pot on the bottom of the pond. If the water is deep, lower the pot on a length of string.

Bog Plants

Planting a bog garden beside a pond simply involves bringing the liner up and over the edge of the pond and extending it under the soil for a distance. You can use the same principle to make a bog garden alone, by digging out a bed to a depth of at least 30 cm (12 in) and lining the base and sides with a sheet of tough polythene or butyl-rubber pond liner. Puncture the lining sparsely before replacing the soil so that some water can drain away and the bed won't become completely waterlogged and stagnant. Soak the soil thoroughly before planting it up. If you have children, this kind of garden is a safe alternative to a pond while they are young.

plant
alchemy

Companion Planting

Companion planting is one of the mysteries of gardening. It describes the relationship between two species, when growing them together actively benefits one – if not both – of the plants.

In the Vegetable Plot

Various beneficial properties are attributed to French marigolds (*Tagetes patula*). Planting them between rows of potatoes can help limit eelworm damage to the potatoes, because the French marigolds' roots secrete thiophenes – substances that are thought to kill nematodes, particularly eelworms. The plants have the same effect when grown alongside tomatoes. French marigolds reduce whitefly attack, too, and alternating lines of the flowers with rows of cabbages seems to offer this vegetable some protection against brassica whitefly.

Culinary combinations can be effective as growing companions. For example, peppers (*Capsicum*) will suffer less from aphid attack if underplanted with basil. In addition, there is some evidence to suggest that peppers can themselves be useful companion plants. Their root secretions seem to protect plants such as runner beans and peas from a fungal disease called fusarium wilt.

Scent Warfare

There is a theory that the dreaded carrot fly finds its food plant by smell, and that masking the scent with a more pungent plant, such as onion, can make its task harder. Research suggests that you need at least two – and preferably four – rows of onions between each row of carrots for this method to be effective. There is also some evidence that the procedure prevents onion fly attack, making both plants joint beneficiaries.

Mutual friends

Other companion plants that actually benefit each other include asparagus and tomatoes.

Planting tomatoes out in the asparagus bed after the last spears have been harvested reduces the number of weeds that will become established on the site and compete with the asparagus. Asparagus roots, for their part, appear to secrete substances that control the various soil pests affecting the tomatoes.

Gardeners have long recognized that potatoes and broad beans (fava beans) grown together produce better harvests than if grown in isolation – though, so far, no logical explanation has been found for this. Garden lore also recommends planting a clump of horseradish at each corner of the potato bed for an even better crop. If you try this method, be warned that horseradish is very invasive and will need digging up and reducing each year.

Utilizing Nasturtiums

If whitefly are a problem in the greenhouse, sow some nasturtium seed and let the plants scramble freely over the staging. They should make an appreciable difference to the size of the pest population.

Nasturtiums can also help control aphids on broccoli and woolly aphis on apple trees. If the infestation is already well established, make a 'tea' by infusing nasturtium leaves: cover them with water, bring to the boil, then take off the heat and leave to infuse for 15 minutes or so. Strain, cool and dilute by a ratio of around one part nasturtium 'tea' to four parts water before spraying affected plants.

Plants that Repel Other Plants

If we are prepared to accept that some plants can benefit others, it seems a logical progression that there may be plants that can have a negative effect on neighbouring species.

Although the effects of companion planting are hard enough to quantify, those of allelopathy – the harmful effect of one species on another – are even more difficult to demonstrate. Plants compete naturally for light, water and soil nutrients, so these constraints have to be ruled out before it can be said with any degree of confidence that one species has a detrimental effect on another.

Unexplained and largely unresearched garden examples of allelopathy include the fact that sunflowers and potatoes grown in close proximity appear to stunt each other's growth, while the two herbs basil and rue have an obvious antipathy and should be kept apart in the herb garden.

Some flowers also behave badly when they are cut. Sweet peas, for example, give off minute quantities of ethylene – a gas that hastens ripening and decay, thereby causing other flowers to fade more quickly – and so should not be included in mixed arrangements.

Planting Roses

Never plant a new rose in a bed where roses have been growing as it will fail to thrive. This traditional piece of garden wisdom has been scientifically verified. Known as specific replant disease, it is caused by secretions from rose roots, which adversely affect newly planted specimens. Either leave the bed fallow for at least two years or replace the soil.

Insect-Attracting Plants

Aphid-Eaters

Populations of greenfly, which ravage roses, and blackfly, which decimate broad beans (fava beans), can be significantly reduced by encouraging predatory insects to feed on them. Hoverfly larvae are voracious consumers of aphids – a single larva will have eaten up to 600 before it metamorphoses into an adult fly. To build up the hoverfly population you need to start by attracting adults, which feed on nectar and pollen. Unlike, say, bees, hoverflies do not have long probosces, so they can only feed from simple, open flowers.

Members of the umbellifer family are ideal. These are plants with flat, open heads composed of hundreds of tiny flowers. They include angelica (*Angelica archangelica*), yarrow (*Achillea millefolium*), cow parsley (*Anthriscus sylvestris*), dill (*Anethum graveolens*) and fennel (*Foeniculum vulgare*). Fennel is extraordinarily popular with insects of all kinds. Experiments have recorded nearly 500 different species that feed on its flowers, including tiny parasitic wasps whose larvae feed on aphids and caterpillars.

Ladybirds

Adult ladybirds (ladybugs) and their larvae both feed on aphids. Early in the year when the first ladybirds are abroad, aphids can be scarce. But one of the first plants to become infested with aphids is the nettle. By leaving a patch of nettles in a corner you can provide a vital early food source for ladybirds. Later on, when the garden is in full bloom, cutting down the nettles ensures that they move on to help out on other garden plants.

Adult ladybirds overwinter in hollow stems, so it doesn't pay to be too tidy in the garden. Resisting the temptation to chop down spent hollyhock stems could make all the difference to your ladybird population.

Deterring Flies and Other Pests

One country custom to keep flies out of the kitchen is to hang up a large bunch of mint, though it is best to do this before it flowers – or to cut the flower spikes off – as flies are frequent visitors to mint flowers in the herb garden.

Elder leaves are thought to have similar fly-repelling properties and are said to deter wasps, too. In the past, swatches of elder were laid across baskets of soft fruits on their way to market, and strawberry and raspberry containers were edged with twists of the leaves. For obvious reasons, elder bushes were often left to flourish alongside outdoor privies – alongside sweetly scented jasmine – or deliberately set under the windows of farm dairies.

The worst kitchen intruders are cockroaches, but one folk remedy suggests that cockroaches dislike the scent of bay leaves, which should be liberally scattered on kitchen shelves and in cupboards. To deter ants, sprinkle shelves with pennyroyal (*Mentha pulegium*).

Moth Repellents

Elsewhere around the house, clothes moths can be a problem, particularly when woollen fabrics are folded away for the summer and likewise silks and linens during winter. Tried-and-tested moth repellents include dried lavender, sown into traditional cotton bags to avoid scattering loose flowers everywhere. In colder areas, where lavender is hard to grow, dried thyme was sometimes used as a substitute.

Repellents to Rub In

Dried tansy leaves rubbed into a dog's fur will give the animal some protection against fleas. Dried and rubbed leaves of santolina, southernwood, sage and mint can be sprinkled on carpets to drive out carpet beetles.

Labelling Plants

If you've taken a batch of cuttings, one plantlet can look much like another until they begin to grow, especially if you are preparing cuttings from different varieties of one species – fuchsias, for example. This is even more true of hardwood cuttings, which are just so many twigs in the ground until they take. Simple plastic labels with a marker pen will sort them.

Seeds and Herbs

The traditional way to mark rows of seeds – simply piercing the empty seed packet with a twig and pushing this into the end of the row as a temporary marker until the seeds spring up – really can't be improved upon. In the herb garden, similar-looking but different varieties of thyme are worth distinguishing, as are closely related herbs like coriander and chervil. In this case, permanent ornamental markers will look attractive; nostalgic 'heritage' mail order catalogues often have punched zinc or verdigris copper labels to push into the soil, while some potters make terracotta versions incised with names of herbs.

Nursery Labels

Trees and shrubs often come with labels fastened to a branch or stem. If you decide to leave these in place, because the name is particularly difficult or visitors' enquiries get tedious, then check the label regularly, as it can cut into the bark as the tree grows. It may be safer to remove it and paste it into your garden logbook (see page 122) for reference.

Classifying Plants

The system of classification for both plants and animals was developed by the Swedish botanist Linnaeus in the mid-eighteenth century. Some Latin names are obvious: no one will have trouble translating *fragrans* (fragrant), *giganteus* (gigantic), *grandis* (big, showy) or *gracilis* (graceful). Others provide valuable clues to a plant's height and habitat: *repens* means low-growing; oceanicus indicates a seaside plant; *flore pleno* can mean many flowers. More obscure but no less poetic are *flos-cuculi* – flowering when the cuckoo sings – and *mellifera* or honey-bearing. By becoming familiar with a few key Latin names, you can become privy to a true gardening language, an esperanto for passionate gardeners that instantly weeds out the less serious plant lovers.

SUNFLOWERS
Annual sunflowers germinate, grow, flower, produce seed and die all in the space of a year, hence their Latin name *Helianthus annuus*. Cultivars include 'Russian Giant', 'Teddy Bear' and 'Velvet Queen'.

The Language of Flowers

Flowers have had symbolic associations for centuries. Virginal white madonna lilies have long been linked with the Virgin Mary, while red roses have been an enduring symbol of love for almost as long. But it was not until the nineteenth century that a French writer – Charlotte de la Tour – published a complete 'code' of the significance of different flowers.

She explained how feelings and ideas could be expressed by combinations of flowers, leaves, grasses and herbs. This was seized upon with delight by the Victorians with their enthusiasm for sublimating emotion and desire, and it became a language of subterfuge and passion.

Many meanings are logical and easy to trace. Bluebells signify constancy as they continue to flourish despite being picked and trampled. Snowdrops represent hope, because they flower in late winter and remind us of the coming spring. Opium poppies symbolize sleep because of their narcotic sap. And twisting, climbing honeysuckle indicates the ties of love.

Common Flower Meanings

Lavender: Refusal

Narcissus: Egotism

Primrose: Emerging love

Lily of the valley: Friendship

Christmas rose: Anxiety

Sweet william: Fun

Tansy: Rejection

Peony: Contrition

Oak leaves: Take courage

Pimpernel: Let's meet

Orchid: Luxury

Keeping a Garden Logbook

A garden logbook can take its place alongside the most essential tools, and if kept up to date and annotated with honesty, it is guaranteed to improve your success rate with growing flowers and vegetables as the years go by.

Different layouts and styles of logbook-keeping will appeal to gardeners whose priorities are different. Vegetable growers will appreciate quite a scholarly diary with pages marked into columns to record sowing dates, weather conditions, maybe even soil temperatures. Pages of graph paper will be useful for drawing up a plan of the vegetable garden and marking on rows of vegetables.

If you have the time, rough sketches made on the back of an envelope can be transferred to the journal proper. Or, if that seems like a waste of effort, the best thing to do is invest in a tough traveller's notebook, the sort with waterproof covers, plus a no-run waterproof pen. There is much to be said for a characterful logbook with battered edges, mud-splashed pages and the odd squashed blackfly. Equally, a pristine journal written from the relative comfort of the kitchen table is just as useful and can be left lying around on the coffee table rather than being relegated to the shed. Look back at it and wonder. You are writing the personal history of your garden.

Directory

Blackwell Products

Rushey Lane
Albrighton
Wolverhampton
WV7 3AD
Tel: (01902) 372446
*Oak barrel water butts
and planters.*

The Centre for Alternative Technology

Machynlleth
Powys SY20 9AZ
Tel: (01654) 702400
http://www.cat.org.uk
*Research centre
dedicated to green living.
Good leaflets available
on making compost.*

Chase Organics

Riverdene Business Park
Molesey Road
Hersham
Surrey KT12 4RG
Tel: (01932) 253666
*Green manure seed
available by mail
order, plus organic
vegetable seed.*

Chiltern Seeds

Bortree Stile
Ulverston
Cumbria LA12 7PB
Tel: (01229) 581137
http://www.chilternseeds
co.uk
*Seeds of wildflowers,
perennials, annuals,
trees, vegetables and
herbs by mail order.*

Countrywide Workshops Charitable Trust

Lord Arthur Rank Centre
Trostre Road
Llanelli
Carmarthenshire
SA14 9RA
Tel: (01550) 720414
*Flower pot brushes, self-
assembly compost bins
that need no nails,
screws or tools, plus
garden furniture.*

David Austin Roses

Bowling Green Lane
Albrighton
Wolverhampton
WV7 3HB
Tel: (01902) 376300
*Old-fashioned roses a
speciality, by mail order.*

**The Dulux Advice
Centre**
ICI Paints
Wexham Road
Slough
Berkshire SL2 5DS
Tel: (01753) 550555
*Contact for advice on
and stockists of Cuprinol
Garden Shades and
Garden Wall Shades, for
adding colour to wood,
concrete, terracotta
and stone.*

Fertile Fibre
Tenbury Wells
Worcestershire
WR15 8LT
Tel: (01584) 781575
*Organic compost and
garden fertilisers by
mail order.*

Garden Systems
I Technical Site
Clopton
Woodbridge
Suffolk IP13 6SW
Tel: (01473) 738280
*Suppliers of the Leaky
Pipe system that uses
permanent porous piping
to water garden soil.
Also sells a range of
greenhouse heaters.*

Green Gardener
41 Strumpshaw Road
Brundall
Norfolk NR13 5PG
Tel: (01603) 715096
*Suppliers of biological
controls for pests by
mail order.*

**Greenacres
Horticultural Supplies**
PO Box 1228
Iver
Buckinghamshire
SL0 0EH
Tel: (01895) 835235
*Suppliers of pre-
germinated lawn seed,
ideal for repairing
grassed areas, by mail
order.*

**The Hardy Plant
Society**
Little Orchard
Great Comberton
Pershore
Hereford & Worcester
WR10 3DP
Tel: (01386) 710317
http://www.hardy-
plant.org.uk
*A society dedicated to
conserving older and
more unusual plants.*

Henry Doubleday Research Association

Ryton Organic Gardens
Ryton-on-Dunsmore
Coventry CV8 3LG
Tel: (01203) 303517
http://www.hdra.org.uk
The national centre for organic gardening – members are kept up to date with magazines and newsletters.Organic seed sold by mail order; free catalogue.

Labelplant

The Old Bakery
Labelplant
Wroxham Road
Poole
Dorset BH12 1NJ
01202 540 678
Plant labels by mail order, including aluminium, copper and scratch-on plastic.

The Milliput Company

Unit 8
The Marian Mawr
Industrial Estate
Dolgellau
Mid Wales LL40 1UU
Tel: (01341) 422562
http:// www.milliput.com
Manufacturers of Milliput epoxy putty for repairing terracotta pots, available by mail order.

The National Council for the Conservation of Plants and Gardens

The Stable Courtyard
Wisley Garden
Wisley
Woking
Surrey GU23 6QP
Tel: (01483) 211465
The charitable organisation that oversees around 600 National Collections of different plant genera.

The National Gardens Scheme

Hatchlands Park
East Clandon
Guildford
Surrey GU4 7RT
Tel: (01483) 211535
http://www.ngs.org.uk
The chance to visit inspirational gardens – many of them private – and raise money for charity. The famous 'yellow book' is published every spring and lists open days gardens open in England and Wales. For details of a separate scheme in Scotland, phone (0131) 229 1870 or visit the website.

Peter Beale's Roses
London Road
Attleborough
Norwich
Norfolk NR17 1AY
Tel: (01953) 454707
*More than 1,100
varieties of rose available
by mail order.*

The Recycle Works
Unit 1
Bee Mill
Ribchester
Nr Longridge
PR3 3X2
Tel: (01254) 820088.
http://www.recycleworks
.co.uk
*Self-assembly wooden
compost bins that need
no nails or screws, plus
wormeries and leaf-
mould composters,
available by mail order.*

**The Royal Horticultural
Society, Membership
Department**
PO Box 313
London SW1P 2PE
Tel: (020) 7821 3000
http:// www.rhs.org.uk

Simpson's Seeds
The Walled Garden
Nursery
Horningsham
Warminster
Wiltshire BA12 7NQ
Tel: (01883) 715242
*Suppliers of seed for
many varieties of
tomatoes, vegetables
and seed potatoes.*

Suffolk Herbs
Monks Farm
Coggeshall Road
Kelvedon
Essex CO5 9PG
Tel: (01376) 572456
Mail order.

Two Wests & Elliot
Unit 4
Carrwood Road
Sheepbridge Industrial
Estate
Chesterfield
Derbyshire S41 9RH
Tel: (01246) 451077
*Mail order catalogue
specialising
in greenhouse and
conservatory equipment.*

Wiggly Wigglers
Lower Blakemere Farm
Blakemere
Herefordshire HR2 9PX
Tel: (01981) 500391
http://www.wiggly
wigglers.co.uk
*Wormeries and compost
bins by mail order.*

Picture Credits

Pia Tryde: page 2

Melanie Eclare: pages 16-17

Huntley Hedworth: page 31

Ian Skelton: page 53

Charlie Colmer: page 58

James Merrell: page 71

Michael Paul:
pages 86-7 and 101

Clay Perry:
pages 104-5 and 118-119

Styling Credits

Ben Kendrick
Hester Page
Gabi Tubbs
Sophie Martell